So You Think You Want to Follow Christ?

Written by Steven E Lindsey
Illustrated/Design Layout by Jan Asleson

Copywrite © 2022 Steven E Lindsey

All rights reserved. No part of this book may be reproduced in any form or by any electronic or mechanical means including information storage and retrieval systems, without permission in writing from the publisher, except by reviewers, who may quote brief passages in review...

ISBN 9798218015367

Library of Congress Control Number 2022910548

THE HOLY BIBLE, NEW INTERNATIONAL VERSION®, NIV® Copyright © 1973, 1978, 1984, 2011 by Biblica, Inc. Used by permission. All rights reserved worldwide.

Printed in the United States of America by Ingram Spark/Lightning Source

Published by Spirit Wings Designs 2022
daslpacker55@yahoo.com

Visit me at www.spiritwingsdesigns.com

So You Think You Want to Follow Christ?

Written
by
Steven E Lindsey

Illustrated by Jan Asleson

This Book Is Dedicated to:

My Mother who read Hulbert's Bible Stories to me as a child, my Grandmother who taught my High School Sunday School Class, my Father who showed me how Christians are to live, my wife Priscilla, who has shown me what unconditional love can be, standing by me daily, and to Jesus Christ, my Savior.

Forward

Congratulations on your journey toward becoming a Christian! I hope to introduce you to the Gospel Message and instruct you in how to respond to Christ's calling and reveal what Blessings you can expect to receive.

I hope to lead you into God's Word, Grace, Baptism, Prayer, Fellowship and more... All critical elements in your journey. Remember, success is in the actual journey, the destination is your ultimate reward...entering into His Kingdom and Glory.

1 Thessalonians 2:12 "...that you would walk worthy of God, who has called you unto His Kingdom and Glory." NKJ

What Is the Gospel?

Basically, the Gospel is the life and character of Christ. The Gospels are the first four Books of the New Testament in the Bible: Matthew, Mark, Luke and John. All these books present the life and character of Christ - God's Son, the King. The Gospels tell of Christ's life on earth - being born of a woman, walking as a man, teaching thousands, being betrayed, murdered, rising from the grave, and walking this earth again before ascending into Heaven to prepare a place for you.

2 Corinthians 4:4 "The god of this age has blinded the minds of unbelievers, so that they cannot see the light of the Gospel that displays the glory of Christ, who is the image of God."

The Trinity

Christ is a part of the Holy Trinity: God, the Father; Christ, the Son; and the Holy Spirit . The Trinity is explained as the three in one. Just as marriage joins two individuals to one union, the Trinity is three persons in one. The Trinity is, was, and always will be. Their presence was in Creation, explained in Genesis, the first Book of the Bible, and can be followed throughout the Bible to Revelation, the last Book of the Bible.

Romans 3:22-24 "This righteousness is given through the faith in Jesus Christ to all who believe. There is no difference between Jew or Gentile, for all have sinned and fall short of the glory of God, and all are justified freely by His grace through the redemption that came by Christ Jesus."

Bowing Before a King

Once you have DECIDED TO FOLLOW JESUS, you will have made the most crucial decision of your life. You have invited the King into your life. Thus, your life must change. In serving a King, one must be obedient to His will. The Bible Scriptures teach us how to be obedient and what God expects from us in our new life. This new life is a process of continual learning, growing, and preparing for the day we can join the King in Heaven. Christ, the King, invites you to be a Child of God. Jesus, Son of God, adopts us into His family as children in Christ. We are unconditionally loved and through Jesus Christ's death, God's Grace is exposed, our sins are forgiven...we are saved from sin. This is Salvation.

1 John 3:1 "See how much our Father loves us, for He calls us His children and that is what we are."

Christ's Death

Are we perfect? No, however, in God's eyes we are. When we accept Christ as our personal Savior, He intercedes for us and presents us to God as Holy, Righteous, and Blameless. This is made possible by His death on the cross. But we will likely continue to sin since we are human. However, through study and with the help of the Holy Spirit, we will grow in our righteousness even though, on our own, we can never be perfect.

1 Corinthians 1:18 "For the message of the cross is foolishness to those who are perishing, but to us who are being saved it is the power of God."

How Do I Respond?

The Scriptures are clear that there is a certain process that needs to be taken to serve the King: **BELIEVE, REPENT, CONFESS, BAPTISM, CHANGE and DISCIPLESHIP.** Salvation is free and given only by the Grace of God. We must act to receive it. Just as Christ had to endure death on the cross, we must act.

John 20:29 "Then Jesus told him, 'Because you have seen Me you have believed; blessed are those who have not seen and yet believe.'"

BELIEVE

CONFESS

REPENT

BAPTISM

Believe

We must believe. We must believe that Christ is King, the Son of God. We must believe that He exists and was born in human form of a virgin woman. We must believe that He lived and died to fulfill prophesy to forgive our sins. We must believe Christ to be the true Son of God and that the Bible is the inspired Word of God. We must believe that Jesus Christ was raised from the dead as witnessed by many and ascended into Heaven where He prepares a place where we can join Him after this life on Earth.

Acts 3:18 "Repent then, and turn to God, so that your sins may be wiped out, that times of refreshing may come from the Lord."

John 3:15 "...that everyone that believes may have eternal life in Him."

Repent

To repent is to recognize that our prior life was not a walk with Jesus and was not following the teachings and examples of Jesus and His Apostles. Repentance is more than a recognition of sin. It includes remorse and the express desire to change your life.

James 5:16 "Therefore confess your sins to each other and pray for each other that you may be healed. The prayer of a righteous person is powerful and effective."

Confession

Once the desire to change is achieved, it becomes necessary to confess publicly that we have sinned, fallen short of God's desires, and truly desire to change our lives and follow the King. This is commonly done before the church body so you can seek their assistance and fellowship.

1 John 1:7 "But if we walk in the light, as He is in the light, we have fellowship with one another, and the blood of Jesus Christ, His Son, purifies us all from sin."

Fellowship

Can a person be a Christian and NOT attend church? That would be difficult. Even in the early church Christians were encouraged to attend fellowship regularly. Fellowship is mutual support. It is a two-way street. One can lean on the other - at times being supported and at other times being the support. We all continually require encouragement and support because satan thrives on wounded Christians. It is extremely easy for new Christians to get caught unaware by satan, so surround yourself with Christian friends and Fellowship, and allow yourself to grow through the challenges.

Ephesians 4:16 "From Him the whole body, joined and held together by every supporting ligament, grows, and builds itself up in love, as each part does its work."

Baptism

Baptism is one of the most significant steps we take as Christians. Baptism is commanded by Christ and was practiced by Christ. It is the complete immersion of the body in water to enact the death, burial, and resurrection of Christ being raised in newness of life. Many have been christened as babies and some feel this is adequate. It is NOT! Christening is not Biblical and cannot be found in Scripture. It has become a tradition in some churches to commit the parents to raising a baby in Christ's teachings. Christening is not the same as Baptism but has been confused with it. Baptism is a personal, voluntary decision by a knowing individual to commit his life to Christ.

Acts 22:16 "Peter replied, 'Repent and be baptized, every one of you, in the name of Jesus Christ for the forgiveness of sins, and you will receive the gift of the Holy Spirit.' "

Some believe that the Holy Spirit enters the body during Baptism. That may well be true. The Holy Spirit does enter the Christian's body (soul) and assists the Christian in facing day to day struggles of life. The Holy Spirit is a part of the Trinity and gives assistance in many ways. You can feel the Holy Spirit direct your life as you read and study Scripture and Fellowship with other Christians.

Baptism is a personal action and is a necessary act to fulfill the commands of the King. It is a serious act and should never be done hastily or on impulse, but only after Scripture study and prayer. Baptism will set you apart from the world and by the help of the Holy Spirit give you strength to combat the pressures of a sinful world.

Romans 6:4 "We were therefore buried with Him through baptism into death in order that, just as Christ was raised from the dead through the glory of the Father, we too may live a new life."

Faith

Faith is knowing, as described in *Hebrews 11:1 "Faith is the assurance of things hoped for and the evidence of things not seen."* It is complete trust and confidence of results without absolute proof. As you read and study Scripture, your Faith will grow. As you analyze and ponder the wonders of Creation, your Faith will grow. It is by your Faith you are saved. It is that initial feeling of needing something bigger than ourselves, bigger than anything we know that leads us to Faith in Jesus Christ.

Matthew 17:20 "He replied, 'Because you have so little faith. Truly I tell you, if you have faith as small as a mustard seed, you can say to this mountain, 'Move from here to there' and it will move. Nothing will be impossible for you.' "

Romans 4:13 "It was not through the law that Abraham and his offspring received the promise that he would be heir of the world, but through the righteousness that comes by faith."

Lord's Supper

"Do this in remembrance of Me" is a command from the lips of our King, Himself. We must share these sacraments on a regular basis if we are to be faithful to Christ's teachings. Not to partake is disobedience, just as taking it with hate in our hearts is to disobey.

"For as often as you eat this bread and drink this cup, you proclaim the Lord's death until He comes."
1 Corinthians 11:26

In Hebrews, "to remember", means more than simply to bring something to mind. It means to totally recapture as much of the reality and significance of an event or experience as possible. To relive the event. To relive Christ's sacrifice on the cross with Him: the agony, the suffering and death, as much as is possible. When we come to the Lord's table - remembering His "once-for-all" sacrifice for us - and we rededicate ourselves to His obedient service. No frequency is given in Scripture, so we can assume it to be a permanent feast proclaiming our love for our Christ and King. Besides being a remembrance, it is a celebration of Christ living eternally and us desiring His future return to take us into His Glory.
1 Corinthians 11:23-24

Luke 22:19 "And He took bread, gave thanks and broke it saying "This is my body given for you; do this in remembrance of me."

Discipleship

Your first response is to witness to others. This is a continual process and never ends. Witness and teach others so that they may, in turn, witness and teach others. You are never finished until Christ takes you home. Your job as a Christian is to introduce others to God's Word. By doing so, you keep God's Word in front of each generation and grow together. The importance is not in numbers but in love. Because we love Christ, we love His creation and want ALL to find the same Blessings we have found in Christ.

Acts 1:8 " But you will receive power when the Holy Spirit comes upon you; and you will be my witnesses in Jerusalem, and in all Judea and Samaria, and to the ends of the earth."

Blessings to Expect

The first Blessing is enjoyed by all, believers and non-believers. That is the Creation: this Earth, the creatures that inhabit it, even the air we breathe. God made it all from nothing, He made it ALL and said, "It is Good." The birds, the sun, the critters, the fish....and MAN. YOU!!! He wants your company and a personal relationship with you. He made Earth for MAN - His crowning Creation. God walked in the coolness of the day with Man and spoke directly to him, until sin entered the world. Sin was by man's choice and has haunted mankind ever since.

Romans 1:20 "For since the creation of the world God's invisible qualities - His eternal power and divine nature - have been clearly seen, being understood from what has been made, so that people are without excuse."

God's Word

Further, believers are blessed by God's Word, the Bible. This book was written by God through the hand of inspired men. It was inspired by God and has been preserved in identical text for thousands of years. It begins with Creation. It tells of early Christians and their struggles and triumphs. It tells of Christ's life and teachings which we call the Gospels. It has preserved the letters the Apostles sent to various newly established churches. Then, it ends with prophecy of what is to come, including the forming of a New World for those who have accepted Christ as their Savior and King. Further, there is a promise, a covenant, that if we accept and believe in Christ, repent, confess, and are baptized we will be part of that new world which Christ is preparing for us today.

Isaiah 40:8 "The grass withers and flowers fall, but the Word of our God endures forever."

Grace

Grace is simply beyond our imagination. God loves you so much that He sent His only Son to this Earth to live as a man, only to be murdered by man so your sins could be forgiven. Further, He raised Christ from the grave to show His Holy Power over death so you can receive life ever-lasting. This Grace is free for the asking but requires our allegiance to the King. Grace is a true gift. It is one of the Blessings you receive by giving your life to Christ.

Romans 3:24 "All are justified freely by His grace through the redemption that came by Christ Jesus."

Prayer

Prayer is communication with God, Jesus and the Holy Spirit. It is a direct connection with God. As a Christian, you can be fearless in God's very presence and be assured you have His full and complete attention. Although the Heavenly Father knows your every need, even before you do, you need to honor and worship your Lord and King, thanking Him for the many Blessings bestowed on you. Always remember that nothing is hidden from God. So, take your every care to Him. Prayer strengthens your relationship and keeps you close in an intimate connection. He desires for you to know Him and learn His nature and the things He loves. Prayer is worship and is an expression of love for the Grace so richly given.

Philippians 4:6 "Do not be anxious about anything, but in every situation, by prayer and petition, with thanksgiving, present your requests to God."

Holy Spirit

The Holy Spirit is a part of the Trinity and is, was and always will be. He becomes a part of you when you accept Christ as your Savior as a new Christian. Some would say the Holy Spirit enters the Christian upon Baptism, but it is enough to say that He is within you as a Christian. He is there. He is your crutch. He is literally your soulmate. He will, when asked, help with decisions, words, and actions.
The Holy Spirit is with you every day and will protect you from satan's deadly grip.

Luke 11:13 "If you then, though you are evil, know how to give good gifts to your children, how much more will your Father in Heaven give the Holy Spirit to those who ask Him!"

Family

Another Blessing is Family. Upon accepting Christ, you are adopted into the Family of God. You are invited to fellowship with all Christians. Fellowship is to support others and be supported by others. Fellowship is so important to keeping yourself in tune with Christ's teachings and learning His Word. As a member of God's Family, you inherit the Kingdom of God by being His very child. You are not just a member of the Kingdom, but you are sons and daughters of the KING. Thereby, you inherit all the Blessings that God's Grace has set aside for His Children.

Galatians 6:10 "Therefore, as we have opportunity, let us do good, to all people, especially to those who belong to the family of believers."

Salvation

We have spoken of salvation several times. Salvation is the promise that your sins are forgiven. It is a covenant between God and Man, that upon accepting Christ, believing, repenting, confessing, being baptized, and following Christ's commands, all our sins will be forgiven. Once you have obeyed these requirements, you can follow Jesus. This decision is a serious one. It is a lifetime commitment. It should not be made in haste or under impulse but after study and even prayer. We are not born Bible scholars, but we are now prepared to learn and move forward as the children of God. You will grow in your faith through prayer, study, and fellowship. You can allow the Holy Spirit to gently lead and advise your daily decisions. You can lean on your church family to help keep satan at bay. And you can pray daily, developing a close, knowing relationship with Christ.

Romans 1:16 "For I am not ashamed of the Gospel, because it is the power of God that brings salvation to everyone who believes, first the Jew, then to the Gentile."

As previously suggested, the decision about becoming a Christian is a process or a journey. Entering into God's Kingdom and His Glory is His ultimate end reward. So, enjoy your trip and may God Bless the journey and your Heavenly Reward!

I pray that this study has been helpful and I pray for your success in this journey you are preparing to travel. Amen

John 3:16 "For God so loved the world that He gave His one and only Son, that whosoever believes in Him shall not perish but have eternal life. For God did not send His Son into the world to condemn the world but to save the world through Him."

Steven E Lindsey
Author

Steven E Lindsey is retired in southeast Kansas. He and wife, Priscilla, have bred, raised, trained and ridden Arabian horses for over forty years for distance events. They have seen a great deal of God's creation from between horses' ears. Steve was a forester professionally, though later in life he worked in the insurance industry as agent, owner, and wholesaler. They have served at several churches in Kansas, Colorado, and Missouri, and are now part of the leadership in a newer plant, Impact Christian Church in Independence, Kansas. Not a pastor, not a priest. Just one of God's servants waiting to join Him in the Kingdom.

You can contact Steve at: lindseyagency@yahoo.com

Jan Asleson - Author/Illustrator

My designs are inspired by a desire to share with others the beauty of God's creation that I see around me. My passion is to encourage others through my artistic mediums to not give up on their dreams, to recognize the Blessings all around them and to know that there is always hope.

I find my creativity in many mediums including watercolor, acrylics, pastels, oils, jewelry design, book illustration work, silk art, metal work, watercolor and portraiture.

I live in South-East Kansas with my husband David.

You can find me at www.spiritwingsdesigns.com

www.ingramcontent.com/pod-product-compliance
Lightning Source LLC
LaVergne TN
LVHW071701060526
838201LV00038B/399